ChatGPT

The Artificial Intelligence of Tomorrow... That's Here Today!

ChatGPT

The Artificial Intelligence of Tomorrow... That's Here Today!

Gary Stevens

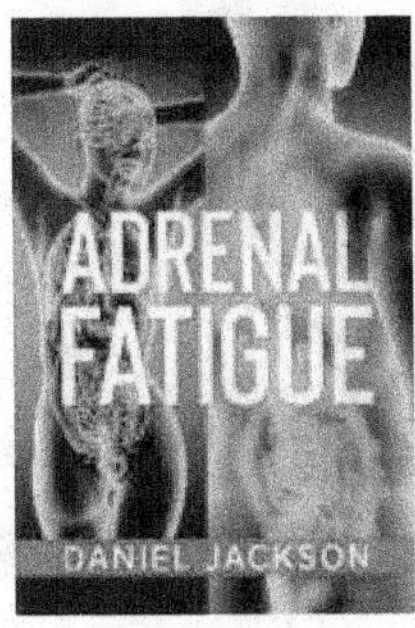

Take a look at more great books available from Rockwood Publishing

... some for FREE!

Just visit the link below:

rockwoodpublishing.co.uk

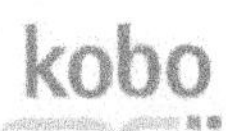

Contents

Introduction: What is ChatGPT and What Can It Do?

ChatGPT is a powerful AI-assisted conversational writing tool that makes it easy to create engaging and high-quality conversations. With ChatGPT, you can quickly create conversations with natural language processing (NLP) capabilities that enable you to generate content at scale.

It provides an intuitive interface for creating and managing conversations, as well as a powerful set of features that allow you to customize the conversation flow.

Whether you're a copywriter or content writer, ChatGPT can help you unleash the power of AI-assisted conversational writing and get more out of your work. This guide will show you how to use ChatGPT for maximum efficiency and effectiveness in your projects.

The beauty of ChatGPT is that it's an AI-assisted _conversational_ writing tool that uses natural language generation to help content writers create engaging conversations. It enables writers to quickly generate conversation scripts for chatbots, virtual assistants, and other interactive applications.

With ChatGPT, content writers can create more natural-sounding conversations faster than ever before. The tool also helps them save time by automating the process of generating conversation scripts from scratch. With its advanced AI capabilities, it can understand the context of a conversation and provide relevant responses in real-time.

ChatGPT is revolutionizing the way we write conversational content and is set to become an invaluable asset for copywriters in the future.

With ChatGPT, you can create conversations, generate articles, and even create personalized messages in a fraction of the time it would take to do manually. This makes it an invaluable asset for content creators who need to produce high-quality content quickly and efficiently.

ChatGPT is a conversational AI builder software that helps businesses create chatbots and other automated conversations. It is a powerful tool that can be used to automate customer service, marketing, sales, and other tasks.

ChatGPT has already been used by many companies to create chatbots for their websites and mobile apps. With its easy-to-use interface and powerful features, it has become one of the most popular chatbot development platforms in the market today.

The model is trained using a technique called unsupervised learning, which means that it is not explicitly provided with correct answers during training. Instead, it learns to generate text that is similar to the text in the training dataset.

Due to its massive training dataset and transformer-based architecture, it can handle a wide range of topics and can generate text that is difficult to distinguish from text written by humans.

Some Applications of ChatGPT

ChatGPT is a powerful language model that can be used for a variety of natural language processing tasks. Beyond the more common applications such as text generation, text completion and summarization, the model has the potential to be used for advanced applications that can have a significant impact in various industries.

One advanced application of ChatGPT is in the field of chatbot development. ChatGPT can be fine-tuned to understand the context of a conversation and generate relevant responses, making it a powerful tool for building chatbots that can have a natural conversation with users. The model can be used to build chatbots for customer service, e-commerce, and other applications where a human-like conversation is required.

Another advanced application of ChatGPT is in the field of question answering. The model can be fine-tuned to understand a question and generate a relevant and accurate answer. This can be used to build question answering systems for a wide range of applications such as customer service, knowledge management, and research.

Another interesting application is in the field of language translation. ChatGPT can be fine-tuned for language translation tasks by training it on a dataset of parallel text in different languages. This can help to improve the quality of machine translation and make it more accessible for a wider range of users.

In the field of creative writing, ChatGPT can be used to generate poetry, song lyrics, scripts, stories and more. With the model's ability to understand context and generate human-like text, it can be a powerful tool for creative writers looking for inspiration or to help generate new ideas.

In the field of data generation, GPT based models can be fine-tuned to generate structured data such as tables, charts, and graphs. This can help to improve the efficiency of data-driven tasks such as data entry, data analysis, and data visualization.

In conclusion, ChatGPT is a powerful language model that has the potential to be used for a wide range of advanced applications beyond the more common natural language processing tasks. By fine-tuning the model for specific tasks, it can have a significant impact in various industries such as chatbot development, question answering, language translation, creative writing and data generation.

Using ChatGPT for fiction and non-fiction book outline creation

ChatGPT can be used for both fiction and non-fiction book outline creation. It uses the latest natural language processing technology to generate ideas and outlines.

It is also very helpful for brainstorming and coming up with creative solutions to story development.

You can start with a prompt, then go back and forth with the model to come up with a detailed outline.
You can also ask the model to turn the conversation into an outline or a specific number of chapters.

Additionally, it can add characters and subplots to give the story more depth.

So the possible process for writing a book/article could look something like this:

- You have an idea for a book topic (or ask ChatGPT to come up with one!)
- Ask ChatGPT to generate an outline for the book (ie relevant topics to be covered in the book, sub-topics, chapter headings, sub-headings etc)
- Put each topic, sub-topic, heading or sub-heading back into ChatGPT and ask it to write x number of words/paragraphs about that topic/sub-topic, heading/sub-heading
- If needs be ask ChatGPT to expand on what it has already come up with (ie additional text) or even re-write it in a different "tone"
- You can even put a whole paragraph that ChatGPT has come up with back into it and ask it to fully expand on it with 10, 20, or 30 more paragraphs (at this point you have to be sure that ChatGPT doesn't start duplicating information/responses)

So you can see just how powerful ChatGPT can be in helping you write articles, blog posts, or even full books… BUT you have to be sure that the content generated is factual, relevant, non-duplicated and very importantly in the "tone" or "voice" that reflects the character and personality of both you and the subject matter.

Writing compelling sales pages with ChatGPT

ChatGPT can be used to great effect to write compelling sales pages.

It can generate ideas and help brainstorm copy, write SEO meta descriptions, create rough outlines for blog posts, and make sure you don't miss any obvious points.

To get the most out of it, it's important to give it direction and ask it for multiple suggestions to A/B test.

You should also give it enough content to work from, such as an entire article, so it can accurately summarize and provide ideas.

Using ChatGPT to leverage social media

Everybody understands just how powerful social media can be to either get your message across, promote your work, build an audience or make money.

The challenge however can be the sheer amount of time it can take to write different posts for different platforms as they all have their own specific requirements and limitations.

ChatGPT knows and understands these requirements and will write posts based on the platform for which you specify.

For example, a LinkedIn post needs to be less than 500 characters (not words) and should also contain any relevant hashtags, but an Instagram caption should be no more than 150 characters and include hashtags _and_ emojis, whereas a Twitter tweet needs to be less than 280 characters.

ChatGPT takes care of all of this for you.

Just put in a piece of your own content, ask it to repurpose it for the relevant social media platform, and then you just post it. Job done!

Using ChatGPT to write interesting and engaging emails

ChatGPT can be used to come up with interesting, personal, and engaging emails. It can generate unique and natural sounding text that can pique the reader's interest.

ChatGPT also uses Reinforcement Learning with Human Feedback (RLHF) to ensure that the text generated is relevant and engaging.

Furthermore, it can also be used to create personalized communication such as email responses and product recommendations.

Coming up with podcast scripts/outlines

You can use ChatGPT to come up with podcast script outlines by asking it to generate episode ideas, titles, outlines, introductions and even outros.
It can provide you with a blueprint that you can use to kickstart a podcast episode.
For example, if you ask ChatGPT to 'Write me a script for a podcast about UFO sightings in Scotland', it will generate a script like the one mentioned in the given text.

Additionally, ChatGPT can help you with top-level research by searching through thousands of online sources to pull out information and present it in a coherent way.

Using ChatGPT to come up with business ideas

You can use ChatGPT to come up with business ideas by first identifying a problem or need in the market that your business can solve.

Once you have identified the need, you can create a business plan, raise capital and start writing.

Additionally, you can use ChatGPT to generate unique and non-plagiarized product descriptions for dropshipping businesses, and you can also use it to start freelance writing.

Using ChatGPT for content creation

Companies can use ChatGPT to assist with content creation by utilizing its natural language processing and GPT-3 technology to generate engaging and relevant content for their target audience.

ChatGPT can help businesses create content that is tailored to the specific interests and needs of their audience and can assist with researching and curating content from various sources.

Additionally, ChatGPT can be used for conversation tasks, such as providing conversation prompts or engaging in social media conversations.

Content marketers can use ChatGPT to help generate ideas, research and curate content, and create content that is tailored to their target audience.

Is ChatGPT better than Google for general inquiries?

ChatGPT can be more useful than Google for general inquiries.
Studies have shown that ChatGPT outperforms Google on coding queries and ties it on general informational queries.

ChatGPT is able to provide more personalized and conversational results and is better at understanding contextual queries.

Additionally, it can provide more contextually relevant responses than Google.

Prompt Engineering

Prompt what?!

(Hint: this does not mean getting a construction job done quickly!)

Prompt engineering is a concept in artificial intelligence, particularly natural language processing, in which the description of the task that the AI needs to complete is carefully crafted to ensure that the AI produces the desired output.

This involves understanding the AI's capabilities and limitations, designing the prompts to be as clear and concise as possible, and testing them to ensure that they yield the desired results.

The quality of input determines the quality of output. Designing effective prompts (commands; questions; directives etc.) increases the probability that you will get a response that is of good quality and that is in context.

Some people like to think of it as being akin to the game "Charades" where the performer provides just enough information for their partner to work out what the word or phrase is.

Think of ChatGPT as being your partner in a game of charades. Just enough information is provided with your prompt for ChatGPT to work out the patterns and come up with the information or outcome that you need.

There is absolutely no point in overloading and overwhelming ChatGPT with all the information at once as this is very likely to interrupt the natural flow of its intelligence and reasoning.

That being said, there obviously needs to be a certain amount of specificity. For example, rather than just asking: "Where do you suggest I take my next vacation?" you would get far more relevant results if you gave some specifics based on your requirements, like: "Where would you suggest as a holiday destination in Europe for two weeks in Summer with a budget of $3500 for two people?" With this prompt, you are specifying where, how long, when, cost and for how many. Obviously, in this scenario, you'd get way more suggestions that would be useful to you.

One last thing about prompts, don't be afraid to have a play around and experiment a little… or a lot! ChatGPT could take you on a journey you'd never have thought about. Some journies may end up in a bit of a one-horse town, but others may end up in a golden city of previously unthought-of possibilities.

The above may sound like I'm talking in opposites, and to a degree I am!

First I say "Be specific", then I say "Experiment". The fact is they're both legitimate methods of using ChatGPT, it all depends on your initial needs, and for what you want ChatGPT to help with.

As the saying goes, "It's all good".

Some people go as far as to say that Prompt Engineering is the "be-all and end-all" of using A.I. in general and that if you get this part right, you're home and dry and good to go with the content that will be generated, and to be honest, there's a LOT of truth in that point of view.

The questions you ask and the way prompts are structured will make the difference between the response generated being either irrelevant nonsense or golden nugget perfection.

It's in effect a skill in its own right and you will get better and better at it the more you work with ChatGPT and hone your prompting abilities.

Developing and Deploying ChatGPT Applications

Developing and deploying ChatGPT applications can be a complex process, but it can also be a powerful way to create innovative and useful tools for a wide range of industries and domains.

One key step in developing a ChatGPT application is to determine the specific task or tasks that the application will be used for. This could be anything from natural language understanding and generation, to machine learning and deep learning, to text summarization and sentiment analysis. Once the task is defined, it is important to gather and prepare a suitable dataset for training the model. This dataset should be large, diverse and labeled, in order to ensure that the model can learn effectively and generalize well to new inputs.

After the model is trained, it is important to evaluate its performance on a held-out test set to ensure that it is working as expected. Common evaluation metrics include accuracy, F1-score, and perplexity. Once the model is trained and evaluated, the next step is to deploy it in a production environment. This typically involves creating an API or web application that allows users to interact with the model and receive results.

Deploying a ChatGPT model can be done in several ways. One common way is to use a cloud-based platform such as AWS, Azure, or GCP to deploy the model as a web service. This allows the model to be easily accessible to users and can also provide scalability and reliability. Another way is to deploy the model on-premises, which may be necessary for organizations that have strict data security requirements.

In addition to deploying the model, it is also important to monitor its performance and make updates as necessary. This could involve retraining the model on new data, adjusting the model architecture, or fine-tuning the model for specific tasks.

Developing and deploying ChatGPT applications can be a complex process, but it can also be a powerful way to create innovative and useful tools for a wide range of industries and domains. It is important to define the specific task, gather and prepare a suitable dataset, evaluate the model's performance and deploy it on a cloud-based platform or on-premises, and monitor its performance and make updates as necessary.

Fine-tuning ChatGPT for specific tasks

Fine-tuning a pre-trained language model like ChatGPT for specific tasks can be a powerful way to improve its performance on those tasks.

The process of fine-tuning involves training the model on a new dataset that is related to the task at hand, while keeping the pre-trained weights of the model as a starting point. This allows the model to leverage its pre-trained knowledge while also learning task-specific information from the new data.

One way to fine-tune ChatGPT is to use a technique called transfer learning. This involves using the pre-trained model as a feature extractor, where the output of the model is used as input to a new model that is trained to perform the specific task. This can be done by adding a new output layer to the pre-trained model and training it on the new dataset.

Another way to fine-tune ChatGPT is to use a technique called end-to-end fine-tuning. This involves training the entire pre-trained model on the new dataset, allowing the model to adjust both its feature extractor and output layers to the task at hand. This method can be more computationally intensive, but it can also lead to better performance on the task.

In order to fine-tune ChatGPT for a specific task, it is important to have a labeled dataset that is representative of the task. This dataset should have a large number of examples, in order to allow the model to learn the nuances of the task. Additionally, it is important to choose an appropriate learning rate and training schedule to ensure that the model can learn effectively from the new data.

Fine-tuning a pre-trained language model like ChatGPT can be a powerful way to improve its performance on specific tasks. This can be done by using transfer learning or end-to-end fine-tuning and it is important to have a good labeled dataset, and appropriate learning rate and training schedule.

Understanding ChatGPT Architecture

ChatGPT is a large language model developed by OpenAI that is based on the transformer architecture.

The transformer architecture is a neural network architecture that was first introduced in a 2017 paper by Google researchers. It has been used in a variety of natural language processing tasks and has become the de facto standard for many state-of-the-art models.

The transformer architecture consists of two main components: the encoder and the decoder. The encoder takes in the input sequence and processes it by passing it through multiple layers of self-attention and feed-forward neural networks.

The self-attention mechanism allows the model to weigh the importance of different parts of the input when making predictions. This allows the model to effectively handle input sequences of varying length and to capture long-range dependencies in the data.

The decoder takes in the encoded input and generates the output sequence. Like the encoder, it also consists of multiple layers of self-attention and feed-forward neural networks.

However, the decoder also includes a mechanism called masking, which prevents the model from seeing the future tokens in the output sequence when generating each token. This helps the model to generate coherent and fluent text.

One of the key strengths of the transformer architecture is its ability to handle input sequences of varying length. Traditional neural network architectures, such as recurrent neural networks, have difficulty handling input sequences that are longer than a few hundred tokens.

The transformer architecture, on the other hand, can handle input sequences of thousands of tokens, making it well-suited for tasks such as language translation and text summarization.

Another strength of the transformer architecture is its ability to capture long-range dependencies in the data.

In traditional neural network architectures, the model can only see a limited context when making predictions.
The transformer architecture, on the other hand, can see the entire input sequence when making predictions, allowing it to capture long-range dependencies that are important for understanding the meaning of the text.

ChatGPT is a powerful natural language processing model developed by OpenAI that is based on the transformer architecture. The transformer architecture is a neural network architecture that is composed of two main components: the encoder and the decoder.

The transformer architecture allows the model to handle input sequences of varying lengths and to capture long-range dependencies in the data. These strengths of the transformer architecture make it well-suited for a variety of natural language processing tasks such as language translation and text summarization.

Integrating ChatGPT with existing systems

Integrating ChatGPT with existing systems can be a powerful way to enhance the capabilities of those systems and improve the user experience. ChatGPT is a large language model that can be used for a wide range of natural language processing (NLP) tasks such as language understanding, generation, and summarization. By integrating ChatGPT with existing systems, it is possible to add NLP capabilities to those systems and make them more intelligent and user-friendly. One common way to integrate ChatGPT with existing systems is to use an API-based approach.

This involves creating an API that allows the existing system to communicate with the ChatGPT model.

The existing system can send text inputs to the API, which will then use the ChatGPT model to process the input and return the results. This approach allows the existing system to access the capabilities of the ChatGPT model without having to make significant changes to the existing codebase.

Another way to integrate ChatGPT with existing systems is to use a plugin or module-based approach. This involves creating a plugin or module that can be added to the existing system.

The plugin or module can access the ChatGPT model and use its capabilities to enhance the existing system. This approach may require more changes to the existing codebase, but it can also provide a more seamless integration with the existing system.

In order to integrate ChatGPT with existing systems, it is important to have a clear understanding of the existing system's architecture and how it interacts with other systems.

This will help to ensure that the integration is done in a way that is efficient and secure. Additionally, it is important to test the integration thoroughly to ensure that it is working as expected.

Integrating ChatGPT with existing systems can be a powerful way to enhance the capabilities of those systems and improve the user experience.

It can be done by using an API-based approach or a plugin or module-based approach. It is important to have a clear understanding of the existing system's architecture, test the integration thoroughly and ensure that the integration is done in a way that is efficient and secure.

Utilizing ChatGPT in Business Applications

ChatGPT is a powerful language model that has the ability to generate human-like text. This makes it a valuable tool for various business applications. One key use case for ChatGPT in business is customer service automation. The model can be trained on a large dataset of customer interactions to understand and respond to customer inquiries.

This allows for efficient and cost-effective customer service, as the model can handle a large volume of interactions simultaneously. Additionally, the model can be programmed to escalate more complex issues to human customer service representatives, ensuring that all customer needs are met.

Another application for ChatGPT in business is content generation. The model can be used to write product descriptions, blog posts, and other marketing materials. This can save significant time and resources for businesses, as the model can generate high-quality content quickly and at scale.

Additionally, the model can be used to generate personalized content for individual customers, increasing the effectiveness of marketing campaigns.

ChatGPT can also be utilized for natural language processing tasks such as sentiment analysis, named entity recognition and language translation. This can help businesses gain insights into customer feedback and improve their products and services.

Overall, ChatGPT has the potential to revolutionize various aspects of business operations. It can increase efficiency, save resources, and provide valuable insights. As the technology continues to evolve, we can expect to see even more innovative uses for ChatGPT in the business world.

ChatGPT is a powerful language model with the ability to generate human-like text. It can be used in a variety of business applications such as customer service automation, content generation, natural language processing, and more. As the technology continues to evolve, we can expect to see ChatGPT being used in even more innovative ways in the future.

Improving ChatGPT Performance

Improving the performance of ChatGPT, a large language model developed by OpenAI, is a crucial task that requires a combination of various techniques. One of the most important ways to improve the performance of ChatGPT is through fine-tuning. Fine-tuning is the process of using a pre-trained model and adjusting its parameters on a new task or dataset. This allows the model to adapt to the specific task or dataset and improve its performance.

Another way to improve the performance of ChatGPT is through data augmentation. Data augmentation involves creating new training examples from existing ones by applying various techniques such as adding noise, rotating images, or flipping them. By creating new training examples, the model can learn to generalize better and improve its performance.

Another important technique for improving the performance of ChatGPT is through the use of transfer learning. Transfer learning is the process of using the knowledge learned on one task to improve the performance on a different but related task. For example, a pre-trained model on a language task can be used as the starting point for a new language task, allowing the model to make use of the knowledge learned on the first task to improve its performance on the second task.

In addition to these techniques, it is also important to use a large and diverse dataset when training ChatGPT.

A large and diverse dataset allows the model to learn from a wide range of examples and improve its performance. Furthermore, it is important to use a high-quality dataset that is free of errors and biases.

Finally, regularization is also an important technique for improving the performance of ChatGPT. Regularization is the process of adding constraints to the model to prevent overfitting.

Overfitting occurs when a model is trained on a limited dataset and becomes too specialized to that dataset, resulting in poor performance on new data. Regularization techniques such as dropout and weight decay can be used to reduce overfitting and improve the performance of the model.

Improving the performance of ChatGPT requires a combination of various techniques such as fine-tuning, data augmentation, transfer learning, using a large and diverse dataset, and regularization. By implementing these techniques, we can improve the performance of ChatGPT and make it more effective in various language tasks.

Troubleshooting ChatGPT Issues

ChatGPT is a powerful language model developed by OpenAI that can generate human-like text. However, like any technology, it can sometimes experience issues that need to be troubleshot. This essay will outline some common ChatGPT issues and provide solutions for resolving them.

One of the most common issues is that ChatGPT may generate nonsensical or irrelevant responses. This can be caused by a lack of context or the model being trained on a dataset that is not relevant to the task at hand. To resolve this issue, it is important to provide as much context as possible and fine-tune the model using a relevant dataset.

Another issue that may arise is that ChatGPT may generate repetitive or generic responses. This can be caused by the model not having enough training data or the training data being too similar. To resolve this issue, it is important to provide the model with a diverse set of training data and fine-tune the model using a relevant dataset.

A third issue that may arise is that ChatGPT may not understand certain words or phrases. This can be caused by the model not being trained on a diverse dataset or not being fine-tuned for a specific task.

To resolve this issue, it is important to fine-tune the model using a relevant dataset and provide it with additional training data that includes the specific words or phrases.

Lastly, ChatGPT may generate text that is grammatically incorrect or has spelling errors. This can be caused by the model not being trained on a diverse dataset or not being fine-tuned for a specific task.

To resolve this issue, it is important to fine-tune the model using a relevant dataset and provide it with additional training data that includes grammatically correct and well-spelled text.

ChatGPT is a powerful language model that can generate human-like text. However, it may experience issues such as generating nonsensical or irrelevant responses, repetitive or generic responses, not understanding certain words or phrases, or generating text that is grammatically incorrect or has spelling errors.

By providing the model with a relevant dataset, additional training data, and fine-tuning it for a specific task, these issues can be resolved.

ChatGPT Security and Privacy Considerations

ChatGPT, a large language model developed by OpenAI, is a powerful tool for natural language processing and understanding. However, like any technology, it also poses certain security and privacy considerations that must be taken into account when using it.

One major concern is the potential for misuse of the model. ChatGPT has the ability to generate human-like text, which could be used to create convincing phishing attempts or impersonate individuals online. Additionally, the model's ability to understand and respond to natural language input could be used for malicious purposes, such as creating chatbots that spread disinformation or engage in cyberbullying.

Another concern is the potential for data breaches. ChatGPT is trained on a massive amount of text data, which includes sensitive information such as personal details and financial information. A breach of the model's data could lead to the exposure of this information to unauthorized parties.

Privacy is also a concern when using ChatGPT. The model's ability to understand and respond to natural language input means that it may be able to extract personal information from users, such as their name, address, or contact details. This information could then be used for targeted advertising or other forms of unwanted communication.

To mitigate these security and privacy risks, it is important to take a number of precautions when using ChatGPT. First, organizations should implement strict access controls to ensure that only authorized individuals have access to the model and its data. Additionally, it is important to regularly monitor the model's output to detect and prevent any misuse or abuse.

It is also essential to implement robust data security measures to protect the model's data from breaches. This may include encryption, regular backups, and the use of firewalls and intrusion detection systems.

Finally, organizations should be transparent about their use of ChatGPT and provide users with clear explanations of how their data will be used and protected. This could include providing a privacy policy that outlines the types of data that will be collected and how it will be used.

ChatGPT is a powerful tool for natural language processing and understanding, but it also poses certain security and privacy considerations.

Organizations should take steps to mitigate these risks, including implementing strict access controls, monitoring the model's output, implementing robust data security measures, and being transparent about their use of the model. By taking these precautions, organizations can ensure that ChatGPT is used safely and responsibly.

Best practices for using ChatGPT

ChatGPT is a powerful language model developed by OpenAI that can be used for a variety of natural language processing tasks, such as text generation, text completion, text summarization, and language translation. However, to get the best results when using the model, it is important to follow some best practices.

First and foremost, it is important to have a clear understanding of the task you are trying to accomplish. ChatGPT can be fine-tuned for specific tasks by training it on a smaller dataset that is relevant to the task. This process is known as transfer learning and can improve the model's performance on that specific task.

Another important consideration is the quality of the training data. The model's performance will depend on the quality of the training data and the specific task it is being used for. The larger, cleaner, and more diverse the training data, the better the model will perform.

It is also important to keep in mind that ChatGPT is not capable of understanding the full context of a conversation and does not have the ability to hold a conversation like a human would. While it can understand context to some degree, it is not a true AI.

When using ChatGPT for generating text, it is important to provide a clear and specific prompt. The more specific the prompt, the more relevant the generated text will be. It's also important to evaluate the generated text and make sure it makes sense and is grammatically correct.

Another important aspect is to be conscious of the ethical and social implications of using such a model. While the model can generate human-like text, it is important to remember that the text is generated by a machine and may not align with human values or ethical standards.

Lastly, it is important to keep in mind the computational resources required to run ChatGPT. Running the model requires a significant amount of computing power, as the model has billions of parameters. It is recommended to use a powerful GPU or cloud-based infrastructure to run the model.

ChatGPT is a powerful language model that can be used for a variety of natural language processing tasks.

By following best practices such as understanding the task, using quality training data, providing clear prompts, and being aware of ethical and computational considerations, users can get the best results when using ChatGPT.

Tips and Tricks for fine-tuning ChatGPT

Fine-tuning ChatGPT for specific tasks is a powerful way to improve the model's performance and make it more useful for a particular application.

However, fine-tuning can be a complex process and there are a few tips and tricks to keep in mind to achieve the best results.
The first tip is to select the right dataset for fine-tuning.

The dataset should be relevant to the task you are trying to accomplish and should be large enough to provide the model with enough examples to learn from. The larger, cleaner, and more diverse the dataset, the better the model will perform.

Another tip is to experiment with different fine-tuning techniques. There are a variety of techniques that can be used to fine-tune the model, such as transfer learning, which involves training the model on a smaller dataset that is relevant to the task, or pre-training, which involves training the model on a large dataset before fine-tuning it on a smaller dataset.

It is also important to experiment with different fine-tuning configurations. For example, adjusting the learning rate, the batch size, and the number of training iterations can have a significant impact on the model's performance.

It's also crucial to monitor the model's performance during the fine-tuning process. Keeping track of metrics such as accuracy, loss, and perplexity can help you to identify when the model has reached its best performance and to understand the impact of different fine-tuning configurations.

Another useful trick is to use pre-trained weights from a similar task. You can use pre-trained weights as a starting point and fine-tune them further on your task-specific dataset. This can speed up the fine-tuning process and improve the model's performance.

Finally, it is important to be aware of the limitations of the model and to interpret the results with caution. The model's output may not always align with human values or ethical standards and should be reviewed by a professional before use. Fine-tuning ChatGPT for specific tasks is a powerful way to improve the model's performance and make it more useful for a particular application.

By selecting the right dataset, experimenting with different fine-tuning techniques, monitoring the model's performance, using pre-trained weights and being aware of the limitations, users can achieve the best results when fine-tuning ChatGPT.

ChatGPT and Explainable AI

ChatGPT is a powerful language model that can be used for a variety of natural language processing tasks, such as text generation, text completion, text summarization, and language translation. However, as a machine learning model, it is important to consider the limitations of the model and its ability to provide explainable AI.

Explainable AI refers to the ability of a model to provide clear and interpretable explanations for its predictions or decisions. This is important for many applications, such as those in healthcare, finance, and other domains where transparency and accountability are critical.

ChatGPT, like other transformer-based models, is based on a neural network architecture and is trained on large amounts of data. It is able to generate human-like text by combining patterns and information it has learned from the training data. However, the model's internal workings are complex and it can be difficult to understand how it arrived at a particular prediction or decision.

One approach to making ChatGPT more explainable is to use techniques such as attention visualization, which can provide insight into which parts of the input the model is focusing on when making a prediction. Another approach is to use methods such as saliency maps, which can highlight the most important input features that the model is using to make a prediction.

Another approach is to use post-hoc methods such as LIME (Local Interpretable Model-Agnostic Explanations) or SHAP (SHapley Additive exPlanations) to explain the model's predictions in a human-readable way.

These methods can provide insights into the model's decision-making process and help to identify the most important features that the model is using to make a prediction.

Another way to increase the explainability of ChatGPT is to use simpler models like rule-based systems, decision trees, or linear models. These models are easier to understand and interpret, but they may not perform as well as ChatGPT on certain tasks.

ChatGPT is a powerful language model that can be used for a variety of natural language processing tasks. However, as a machine learning model, it can be difficult to understand how it arrived at a particular prediction or decision.

To increase the explainability of ChatGPT, it is important to use techniques such as attention visualization, saliency maps, post-hoc methods such as LIME or SHAP, or simpler models. This will help to increase the transparency and accountability of the model's predictions, which is important for many applications.

ChatGPT and Fairness and Bias

ChatGPT is a powerful language model developed by OpenAI that can be used for a variety of natural language processing tasks, such as text generation, text completion, text summarization, and language translation. However, it is important to consider the potential for fairness and bias when using the model.

Fairness and bias in machine learning refers to the potential for a model to make decisions or predictions that are discriminatory or unfair towards certain groups of people. This can happen when a model is trained on biased data or when it is designed with a bias towards certain groups of people.

ChatGPT is trained on a massive dataset of internet text, which can contain biases and stereotypes.

For example, if the dataset contains a disproportionate number of examples of a certain group of people, the model may learn to generate text that reinforces stereotypes about that group.

Additionally, if the dataset contains biased or stereotypical text, the model may generate similar text when making predictions.

To mitigate fairness and bias in ChatGPT, it is important to use diverse, high-quality training data that is free of biases and stereotypes.

Additionally, it's important to fine-tune the model on task-specific data that is representative of the population it will be serving.

Another way to mitigate fairness and bias in ChatGPT is to use techniques such as fairness constraints or pre-processing methods, which can help to balance the representation of different groups of people in the training data.

It is also important to evaluate the model's performance on a diverse set of test data and to monitor its performance over time.
This can help to identify any issues with fairness or bias and to make adjustments to the model as needed.

ChatGPT is a powerful language model that can be used for a variety of natural language processing tasks. However, it is important to consider the potential for fairness and bias when using the model.

To mitigate fairness and bias in ChatGPT, it is important to use diverse, high-quality training data, fine-tune the model on task-specific data, use techniques such as fairness constraints or pre-processing methods, evaluate the model's performance on a diverse set of test data, and monitor its performance over time.

ChatGPT and the Human-in-the-loop

ChatGPT is a powerful language model developed by OpenAI that can be used for a variety of natural language processing tasks, such as text generation, text completion, text summarization, and language translation. One approach to using the model is to incorporate human input into the process, known as "human-in-the-loop" or HITL.

The human-in-the-loop approach involves incorporating human input into the decision-making process of the model. This can be done by having a human review the model's predictions before they are used, or by having a human provide feedback to the model during the training process.

One benefit of the human-in-the-loop approach is that it can help to improve the model's performance by providing it with additional information or context that it may not have been able to learn from the training data alone. Additionally, it can help to mitigate any fairness and bias issues that may arise when using the model.

Another benefit of the human-in-the-loop approach is that it can help to ensure the safety and ethical use of the model. By having a human review the model's predictions or provide feedback during the training process, it can help to ensure that the model is not generating harmful or biased text.

There are several ways to implement the human-in-the-loop approach when using ChatGPT. For example, in text generation tasks, the model can generate text, and a human can review and edit the text before it is used. In text summarization tasks, the model can generate a summary, and a human can review and edit the summary before it is used.

It's also possible to use human feedback to improve the model during the training process. For example, a human can provide feedback on the model's predictions, and this feedback can be used to update the model's parameters.

ChatGPT is a powerful language model that can be used for a variety of natural language processing tasks. One approach to using the model is to incorporate human input into the process, known as "human-in-the-loop" or HITL.

This approach can help to improve the model's performance, ensure the safety and ethical use of the model and ensure that the model is not generating harmful or biased text.

There are several ways to implement the human-in-the-loop approach when using ChatGPT, such as having a human review or edit the model's predictions or providing feedback.

ChatGPT and Privacy-preserving techniques

ChatGPT is a powerful language model developed by OpenAI that can be used for a variety of natural language processing tasks, such as text generation, text completion, text summarization, and language translation.

However, when using the model, it is important to consider the potential privacy implications and to use privacy-preserving techniques to protect sensitive data.

Privacy-preserving techniques refer to methods used to protect sensitive data and personal information when using machine learning models. These techniques can be used to protect the privacy of individuals whose data is used to train or test the model, or to protect the privacy of individuals whose data is used as input to the model.

One privacy-preserving technique that can be used when using ChatGPT is differential privacy.

This technique involves adding noise to the data used to train the model, which makes it more difficult for an attacker to infer sensitive information about individuals from the model's output.

Another privacy-preserving technique that can be used is federated learning. This technique involves training the model on decentralized data, rather than on a centralized dataset. This can help to protect the privacy of individuals whose data is used to train the model, as their data is not collected or stored in a centralized location.

Another technique is to use homomorphic encryption, which allows computations to be performed on encrypted data without the need to decrypt it first. This can be used to protect sensitive data when using the model, as the data remains encrypted throughout the process.

It is also important to consider the use of data anonymization and data masking techniques to protect the privacy of individuals whose data is used as input to the model.

ChatGPT is a powerful language model that can be used for a variety of natural language processing tasks. However, when using the model, it is important to consider the potential privacy implications and to use privacy-preserving techniques to protect sensitive data.

These techniques include differential privacy, federated learning, homomorphic encryption, data anonymization and data masking.

By using these techniques, it is possible to protect the privacy of individuals whose data is used to train or test the model, or to protect the privacy of individuals whose data is used as input to the model.

How to use ChatGPT to make money

ChatGPT is a powerful natural language processing model that can be used in a variety of ways to make money. One of the most obvious ways is through the creation of chatbots or virtual assistants. These can be used to automate customer service or sales interactions, allowing businesses to handle a larger volume of inquiries and interactions without needing to hire additional staff.

Another way to use ChatGPT to make money is through content creation. The model can be fine-tuned to generate high-quality, unique content for a variety of purposes. For example, it can be used to create articles for websites, blog posts for businesses, or even entire books. This can be a valuable service for businesses, marketers, or even individual authors looking to save time and effort on content creation.

Another way is through language model fine-tuning, where businesses can fine-tune the model to improve its performance on specific tasks, such as customer service interactions or product descriptions. This can be a valuable service for businesses looking to improve their natural language processing capabilities.

One more way to use ChatGPT to make money is through automated writing and editing services. For example, the model can be used to write emails, social media posts, or even code. Additionally, it can be used to proofread and edit text, helping businesses to improve the quality of their communications and presentations.

Additionally, ChatGPT can be used for natural language processing research, which can be a potential source of revenue for researchers and institutions. The model can be used to conduct experiments and develop new language-based technologies that can be commercialized.

It's worth noting that with any application using GPT-3 or similar AI models, it is important to consider any ethical and legal considerations. For example, if the model is used to generate content for publication or sale, it's important to ensure that the generated content is original and that any necessary permissions have been obtained.

Additionally, any sensitive information generated by the model should be handled appropriately to protect user privacy.

Whether it's through chatbots and virtual assistants, content creation, fine-tuning services, or automated writing and editing, the model has the potential to save businesses time and effort while also improving the quality of their communications and interactions.

You can develop chatbot applications using the ChatGPT model and sell or license them to businesses or individuals.

You can also offer consulting or development services to help others integrate the ChatGPT model into their own projects or products. Additionally, you can create and sell training data to improve the performance of the ChatGPT model on specific tasks or industries. You can also use ChatGPT to generate unique and engaging content for social media, blogs, or websites and monetize that content through advertising or sponsored posts.

You can use ChatGPT to develop automated trading or investment strategies and monetize through trading or consulting. You can also create a subscription-based service where users pay to access a chatbot developed with ChatGPT for customer service, virtual assistance, or other tasks.

You can also offer a language model-as-a-service (LMaaS) where businesses pay to use your ChatGPT model for specific tasks such as language translation, text summarization, and more.

Another way to make money with ChatGPT is through marketing campaigns. With the help of ChatGPT, businesses can create automated marketing campaigns that can reach out to customers in real-time and generate more leads.

ChatGPT can also be used to increase customer loyalty and retention. By providing customers with engaging conversations, they are more likely to stay loyal to the brand. ChatGPT can also be used to target potential customers and increase the reach of the brand. Businesses can create automated campaigns to reach out to potential customers and generate more leads.

Additionally, businesses can use ChatGPT to collect customer feedback and use it to optimize their products and services. This can help improve customer satisfaction and generate more repeat purchases.

Businesses can use ChatGPT to create content for social media and other digital channels to increase brand awareness and engagement.

What about creating codes? ChatGPT can also be used to create discount codes and other offers. Businesses can use ChatGPT to create automated campaigns that offer customers special discounts or coupons.

This can help encourage customers to make purchases and generate more revenue. Additionally, businesses can use ChatGPT to create loyalty programs for their customers. By providing customers with rewards for repeat purchases, this can help increase customer loyalty and retention.

Can ChatGPT write API codes? Yes, ChatGPT can be used to automate the creation of API codes, which can then be used to integrate the ChatGPT platform into other applications and systems. The API codes generated can be used to access the ChatGPT platform, create automated conversations, and manage customer profiles. Additionally, the API codes can be used to create custom applications that can be used to further extend the capabilities of the ChatGPT platform.

What about API codes that can be applied to Facebook? Yes, ChatGPT can be used to create API codes that can be used to integrate the platform with Facebook. This can be done by creating an automated conversation to connect with customers on Facebook and manage customer profiles.

Additionally, the API codes can be used to create automated campaigns that can be used to target potential customers on Facebook and generate more leads. Finally, the API codes can be used to create custom applications that can be used to further extend the capabilities of the ChatGPT platform on Facebook.

Step-by-step instructions on how to make money using AI

1. Research the AI market: Before you start making money with AI, you need to understand the market and the potential opportunities available. Consider researching the current state of the AI market and the types of businesses and projects that use AI.

2. Identify and understand potential AI applications: Once you have a better understanding of the AI market, it's time to start brainstorming potential applications for AI, such as computer vision, natural language processing, and machine learning.

3. Develop an AI solution: Once you have identified potential AI applications, you need to develop an AI solution to address a particular problem. This could involve designing and building a custom AI solution or leveraging existing AI platforms and services.

4. Market your AI solution: Once you have developed your AI solution, you need to find customers who are interested in using it. This could involve creating a website to showcase your AI solution, reaching out to potential customers via email or social media, or attending events to meet potential customers in person.

5. Monetize your AI solution: Once you have identified potential customers for your AI solution, it's time to start making money. This could involve charging customers a one-time fee for your AI solution, or setting up a subscription model where customers pay a recurring fee. Alternatively, you could also look into monetizing your AI solution through advertising or data monetization.

Conclusion and future directions

ChatGPT is a powerful language model developed by OpenAI that can be used for a variety of natural language processing tasks, such as text generation, text completion, text summarization, and language translation. The model has been trained on a massive dataset of internet text, which allows it to generate human-like text by combining patterns and information it has learned from the data.

The model's ability to understand context and generate human-like text has made it a popular choice for a wide range of applications, such as chatbot development, question answering, language translation, creative writing, and data generation. Additionally, the model's ability to be fine-tuned for specific tasks has made it a powerful tool for improving the performance of these applications.

However, there are also several important considerations to keep in mind when using ChatGPT. The model's output may not always align with human values or ethical standards, and it is important to be aware of the ethical and social implications of using such a model. Additionally, the model's performance is heavily dependent on the quality of the training data, and it is important to use diverse, high-quality training data that is free of biases and stereotypes.

Another important consideration is the explainability of the model, which refers to its ability to provide clear and interpretable explanations for its predictions or decisions. ChatGPT, like other transformer-based models, is based on a neural network architecture and is trained on large amounts of data, which makes it difficult to understand how it arrived at a particular prediction or decision.

To increase the explainability of ChatGPT, it is important to use techniques such as attention visualization, saliency maps, post-hoc methods such as LIME or SHAP, or simpler models.

Additionally, when using the model, it is important to consider the potential for fairness and bias, which refers to the potential for a model to make discriminatory or unfair decisions or predictions towards certain groups of people. To mitigate fairness and bias in ChatGPT, it is important to use diverse, high-quality training data and fine-tune the model on task-specific data that is representative of the population it will be serving.

Techniques such as fairness constraints or pre-processing methods can also be used to balance the representation of different groups of people in the training data. It is also important to evaluate the model's performance on a diverse set of test data and to monitor its performance over time.

Furthermore, privacy is also an important consideration when using ChatGPT. Privacy-preserving techniques such as differential privacy, federated learning, and homomorphic encryption can be used to protect sensitive data and personal information when using the model.

Additionally, data anonymization and data masking techniques can be used to protect the privacy of individuals whose data is used as input to the model.

ChatGPT is a powerful language model that has the potential to be used for a wide range of natural language processing tasks. However, it is important to be aware of the ethical and social implications of using such a model, to use diverse, high-quality training data, and to use techniques to increase the explainability and mitigate fairness and bias and privacy issues.

In the future, advancements in language models such as ChatGPT, may lead to more natural human-like conversations, better understanding of context and emotions, and improved performance on a wide range of tasks.

Frequently asked questions and their answers

1. What is ChatGPT?

   ChatGPT is a large language model developed by OpenAI, based on the transformer architecture. It is trained on a massive dataset of internet text and is able to generate human-like text in a variety of contexts.

2. How does ChatGPT work?

   ChatGPT takes in a prompt, or a piece of text that serves as a starting point, and generates a response based on the patterns it has learned from the training data. The model uses a combination of neural networks and machine learning techniques to generate text.

3. What can ChatGPT be used for?

   ChatGPT can be used for a variety of natural language processing tasks, such as text generation, text completion, text summarization, and language translation. It can also be used for chatbot development, question answering, and more.

4. What is the difference between ChatGPT and GPT-3?

   GPT-3 is the parent model of ChatGPT. GPT-3 is even more larger than ChatGPT in terms of parameters, and more fine-tuned to a variety of language tasks.

5. How accurate is ChatGPT?

   ChatGPT is considered to be one of the most accurate language models currently available, but like any machine learning model, its performance will depend on the quality of the training data and the specific task it is being used for.

6. Can ChatGPT understand context and have a conversation?

   ChatGPT has been trained on a wide range of internet text and can understand context to some degree. However, it is not capable of understanding the full context of a conversation and does not have the ability to hold a conversation like a human would.

7. Can ChatGPT be fine-tuned for specific tasks?

   Yes, ChatGPT can be fine-tuned for specific tasks by training it on a smaller dataset that is relevant to the task. This process is known as transfer learning and can improve the model's performance on that specific task.

8. Is ChatGPT open source?
Yes, ChatGPT is open source and the code and pre-trained models are available on the OpenAI GitHub repository.

9. Can I use ChatGPT for commercial purposes?
Yes, you can use ChatGPT for commercial purposes, but you will need to follow the OpenAI API terms of service and any applicable laws or regulations.

10. How much computing power is required to run ChatGPT?
Running ChatGPT requires a significant amount of computing power, as the model has billions of parameters. It is recommended to use a powerful GPU or cloud-based infrastructure to run the model.

11. Can ChatGPT generate original content or does it only repeat what it's been trained on?
ChatGPT is trained on a large dataset of internet text, and it can generate original content by combining patterns and information it has learned from the training data. However, it may also repeat or

generate text that is similar to what it has seen during training, depending on the prompt and the task.

12. Can I train my own version of ChatGPT?
Yes, you can train your own version of ChatGPT by using the open-source code and training it on your own dataset. This can help you fine-tune the model for your specific use case or domain.

13. How large is the training data used to train ChatGPT?
The training data used to train ChatGPT is massive, it's in terabytes. It is a combination of internet text, books, articles and various other forms of text.

14. Is ChatGPT capable of understanding and generating different languages?
ChatGPT has been trained on a wide range of internet text, including text in different languages, but it's primary language is English. There are versions of ChatGPT that have been fine-tuned for other languages like French, German, Spanish, Chinese, etc.

15. Can ChatGPT be used to generate code?
While ChatGPT has been trained on a wide range of internet text, it is primarily designed

for natural language processing tasks and may not be well-suited for generating code. However, there are other models like GPT-3 that have been fine-tuned for code generation.

16. Can ChatGPT identify and understand entities and concepts in a text?
ChatGPT is trained to understand patterns in text and can identify entities and concepts to some degree, but it is not specifically designed for named entity recognition or other specific concept understanding tasks.

17. Can ChatGPT generate structured data?
ChatGPT is primarily designed for natural language processing tasks, and it can generate structured data to some degree, but it is not specifically designed for data generation or data generation tasks.

18. Can ChatGPT be used for sentiment analysis?
ChatGPT can be fine-tuned for sentiment analysis by training it on a dataset of labeled text data. Its ability to understand context and sentiment can be improved by fine-tuning it on sentiment-annotated text.

19. Can ChatGPT be used to generate poetry or creative writing?

   ChatGPT has been trained on a wide range of internet text, including poetry and creative writing, so it can generate poetry or creative writing to some degree, but it is not specifically designed for this task.

20. Can ChatGPT be used to generate legal or financial documents?

   ChatGPT can be fine-tuned for specific use cases such as generating legal or financial documents by training it on a dataset of relevant text. However, it is important to keep in mind that the model's output may not be legally or financially binding and should be reviewed by a professional before use.

Section B: In the Style of Text and Bullet Points

(For those who prefer a more "concise" style of writing and information gathering, this section is aimed primarily at those more involved with I.T., coding, and academia)

Chapter 1: Introduction to ChatGPT

ChatGPT is a variant of the GPT (Generative Pre-training Transformer) language model developed by OpenAI. It is a deep learning model trained on a large dataset of human-generated text, allowing it to generate human-like responses to prompts.

The model is trained using a variant of the transformer architecture, which uses self-attention mechanisms to weigh the importance of different parts of the input when generating a response.

This allows the model to effectively handle input of varying lengths and to understand the relationships between words in a sentence.

ChatGPT is fine-tuned on conversational datasets, allowing it to generate more human-like and context-aware responses in a conversational setting.

It can be fine-tuned on a specific task or used to generate text in various forms, such as chatbot responses, story generation, and text completion.

It has been trained on a large corpus of internet text and has the ability to generate a wide range of human-like text, however it is not infallible and may generate text that is nonsensical or biased.

It is important to note that ChatGPT is a machine learning model, and it is only as good as the data it was trained on. Therefore, biases present in the training data will also be present in the model's output.

Chapter 2: Understanding ChatGPT Architecture

ChatGPT is based on the transformer architecture, which is a type of neural network architecture designed for processing sequential data, such as text. The transformer architecture was introduced in the paper "Attention Is All You Need" by Google researchers in 2017.

The transformer architecture is composed of an encoder and a decoder, which are made up of multiple layers of self-attention and fully connected neural network layers.

The encoder takes in the input text and generates a set of hidden states, which are then passed to the decoder. The decoder uses these hidden states, along with its own internal state, to generate the output text.

The key innovation of the transformer architecture is the use of self-attention mechanisms, which allow the model to weigh the importance of different parts of the input when generating the output. This allows the model to effectively handle input of varying lengths and to understand the relationships between words in a sentence.

In ChatGPT, the encoder is composed of multiple layers of a transformer block, which is made up of a multi-head self-attention mechanism, a feed-forward neural network, and layer normalization. The decoder is similar to the encoder, with the addition of a masked self-attention mechanism, which is used to prevent the model from "cheating" by looking at the future tokens during text generation.

Overall, the architecture of ChatGPT allows it to effectively process and understand sequential data, such as text, making it suitable for tasks such as text generation, conversation, and text completion.

One of the most common applications of ChatGPT is in chatbots. A chatbot is a computer program that simulates conversation with human users. By using ChatGPT, developers can create chatbots that can understand and respond to a wide range of user inputs in a more natural way.

Another application of ChatGPT is in text generation. The model can be fine-tuned to generate text in different styles or formats, such as news articles, stories, or poetry.

It also could be used in text completion, where the model can predict the next word or phrase in a sentence based on the context.

It's important to note that ChatGPT is a machine learning model, which means it can make mistakes or generate nonsensical text. Additionally, since the model is trained on text from the internet, it may contain biases present in the training data. So, It's important to be aware of these limitations when using ChatGPT and to use the appropriate techniques to mitigate them.

Chapter 3: Developing and Deploying ChatGPT Applications

Developing and deploying ChatGPT applications typically involves the following steps:

1. Fine-tuning the model: ChatGPT is a pre-trained model that can be fine-tuned on specific tasks or datasets. This process involves training the model on a smaller dataset that is specific to the task at hand. This allows the model to learn the specific characteristics of the task and generate more accurate and relevant responses.

2. Building the application: Once the model is fine-tuned, it can be integrated into an application. This typically involves building a user interface (UI) that allows users to interact with the model and a back-end that handles the communication between the UI and the model.

3. Deploying the application: After the application is built, it can be deployed in a variety of ways, depending on the specific requirements of the application. For

example, it can be deployed as a web application, a mobile application, or a chatbot integrated with a messaging platform.

4. Monitoring and maintenance: After the application is deployed, it is important to monitor its performance and make adjustments as needed. This includes monitoring the model's accuracy, response time, and user engagement, as well as addressing any bugs or issues that arise.

It is also important to keep in mind that ChatGPT is a deep learning model, which requires significant computational resources to run. It's recommended to use a cloud-based service like OpenAI GPT-3 or Hugging Face to deploy the model. It can also be deployed in a local environment, but it would require a powerful GPU and a high-performance machine.

Additionally, it's important to keep in mind the ethical considerations when deploying ChatGPT-based applications, such as ensuring fair and unbiased results, and making sure that the user's data is handled securely and responsibly.

Chapter 4: Integrating ChatGPT with Existing Systems

Integrating ChatGPT with existing systems typically involves connecting the pre-trained model to the system's API (Application Programming Interface) which allows other programs to communicate with the model.

Here are a few steps that can be followed to integrate ChatGPT with existing systems:

1. Accessing the API: Depending on the system, there may be a pre-built API available for accessing the model. For example, OpenAI provides an API for accessing the GPT models, including ChatGPT.

2. Building a Wrapper: If the system doesn't provide an API, it may be necessary to build a wrapper that connects the model to the system's API. This typically involves writing code that communicates with the model and the system's API and can be done in any programming language.

3. Fine-tuning the model: Once the model is connected to the system, it can be fine-tuned on specific tasks or datasets specific to the system. This process involves training the model on a smaller dataset that is specific to the task at hand. This allows the model to learn the specific characteristics of the task and generate more accurate and relevant responses.

4. Testing and Deployment: After the model is fine-tuned, it can be tested with the existing system. Once tested, the model can be deployed to the production environment and can be integrated with the existing system's workflows.

It's important to keep in mind that the integration process may vary depending on the specific requirements of the system and the model's capabilities.

Therefore, it's important to thoroughly test the integration before deploying it to a production environment.

Additionally, it's important to consider the ethical considerations when integrating ChatGPT with existing systems, such as ensuring fair and unbiased results, and making sure that the user's data is handled securely and responsibly.

Chapter 5: Working with Natural Language Processing

Natural Language Processing (NLP) is a subfield of Artificial Intelligence (AI) that deals with the interaction between computers and human languages. It involves using techniques from computer science, linguistics, and mathematics to process, analyze, and understand human language.

ChatGPT is an NLP model that uses deep learning techniques to process and generate human-like text. It can be fine-tuned to perform a wide range of NLP tasks, such as:

- Text classification: Assigning predefined categories or labels to a piece of text. For example, determining whether a movie review is positive or negative.
- Named Entity Recognition (NER): Identifying and classifying named entities, such as people, organizations, and locations, in a piece of text.

- Sentiment analysis: Determining the sentiment or emotion expressed in a piece of text, such as positive, negative, or neutral.
- Text summarization: Extracting the most important information from a piece of text and condensing it into a shorter version.
- Language Translation: Translating a text from one language to another.

To work with NLP, it's important to have a good understanding of NLP techniques and technologies, as well as the underlying linguistic and mathematical concepts. It's also important to be familiar with programming languages and tools commonly used in NLP, such as Python and NLTK (Natural Language Toolkit).

Additionally, It's also important to keep in mind that NLP models are only as good as the data they are trained on, therefore, it's important to use high-quality, diverse, and unbiased training data to improve the performance of NLP models.

Chapter 6: Improving ChatGPT Performance

There are several ways to improve the performance of ChatGPT, including:

1. Fine-tuning: One of the most effective ways to improve the performance of ChatGPT is to fine-tune the model on a specific task or dataset. This allows the model to learn the specific characteristics of the task and generate more accurate and relevant responses.

2. Using a larger and diverse dataset: Another way to improve the performance of ChatGPT is to train the model on a larger and more diverse dataset, which can help the model learn a wider range of language patterns and reduce bias.

3. Using a bigger model: OpenAI has released several versions of GPT models with different sizes, GPT-2, GPT-3, GPT-3x, etc. Larger models have been trained on more data and have more parameters, which can lead to better performance.

4. Using a fine-tuned version of the model: Fine-tuning the model on a specific task or dataset will result in a better performance on that task.

5. Using appropriate evaluation metrics: Using the right evaluation metrics is important to measure the performance of the model. It's important to use metrics that are appropriate for the specific task, such as accuracy for classification tasks or BLEU score for machine translation tasks.

6. Ensemble methods: Using ensemble methods like using a combination of multiple models or using a combination of multiple outputs from the same model can lead to better performance.

7. Using Transfer learning: Pre-training a model on a large dataset and then fine-tuning it on a specific task can lead to a better performance than training a model from scratch on the same dataset.

Chapter 7: Troubleshooting ChatGPT Issues

There are several issues that may arise when working with ChatGPT, and here are a few common ones and some possible solutions:

1. Bias in the model's output: ChatGPT is trained on a dataset of text from the internet, which may contain biases. To mitigate this issue, it's important to use diverse and unbiased training data, and also consider using techniques like adversarial training or data pre-processing methods to reduce bias in the model's output.

2. Incorrect or nonsensical output: ChatGPT is a machine learning model, and it may generate incorrect or nonsensical responses. To address this issue, it's important to monitor the model's performance and make adjustments as needed, such as fine-tuning the model on a specific task or dataset.

3. Slow response time: ChatGPT is a deep learning model that requires significant

computational resources to run. This can lead to slow response times, especially when dealing with large inputs or complex tasks. To address this issue, it's important to use a powerful GPU or cloud-based services to run the model and also consider using techniques like model compression or quantization to reduce the model's computational requirements.

4. Limited understanding of context: ChatGPT is trained on a dataset of text from the internet, and it may have difficulty understanding the context of specific tasks or domains. To mitigate this issue, it's important to fine-tune the model on a specific task or dataset, and also consider using techniques like context-aware models or pre-training on domain-specific data.

5. Lack of Explainability: Since ChatGPT is a deep learning model, it can be difficult to understand how it generates its output. To mitigate this issue, it's important to use interpretable models, like decision trees, or use explainable AI techniques like LIME (Local Interpretable Model-Agnostic Explanations)

Chapter 8: Utilizing ChatGPT in Business Applications

ChatGPT can be used in a variety of business applications, including:

1. Chatbots: ChatGPT can be used to create chatbots that can understand and respond to a wide range of user inputs in a more natural way. This can be used for customer service, online sales, or other areas where businesses interact with customers via text-based communication.

2. Text generation: ChatGPT can be fine-tuned to generate text in different styles or formats, such as product descriptions, marketing materials, or email responses.

3. Text completion: ChatGPT can be used to predict the next word or phrase in a sentence based on the context. This can be used in applications such as text prediction in mobile keyboards, email clients, or word processors.

4. Sentiment analysis: ChatGPT can be fine-tuned to determine the sentiment or emotion expressed in a piece of text. This can be used in applications such as social media monitoring, customer feedback analysis, or brand reputation management.

5. Language Translation: ChatGPT can be fine-tuned to translate text from one language to another. This can be used in applications such as customer service, e-commerce or global content creation.

6. Summarization: ChatGPT can be used to extract the most important information from a piece of text and condense it into a shorter version. This can be used in applications such as news summarization, document summarization, or meeting minutes.

It's important to note that ChatGPT is a machine learning model and it is only as good as the data it was trained on.

Therefore, biases present in the training data will also be present in the model's output.

It's important to be aware of these limitations when using ChatGPT and to use the appropriate techniques to mitigate them.

Additionally, it's important to consider the ethical considerations when deploying ChatGPT-based applications, such as ensuring fair and unbiased results and handling user's data securely and responsibly.

Chapter 9: ChatGPT Security and Privacy Considerations

ChatGPT, like other language models, can process and generate sensitive information, such as personal information, financial information, and other private data. Therefore, it is important to consider security and privacy when working with ChatGPT. Here are a few things to keep in mind:

1. Data security: The training data used to train ChatGPT may contain sensitive information, such as personal data. It's important to ensure that this data is stored and transmitted securely, and that appropriate access controls are in place to prevent unauthorized access.

2. Model security: The pre-trained models and fine-tuned versions of ChatGPT can be used to generate sensitive information. It's important to ensure that the models are stored and transmitted securely, and that appropriate access controls are in place to prevent unauthorized access.

3. Inference security: ChatGPT can be used to generate sensitive information, such as personal data, financial data, or confidential business information. It's important to ensure that the input data is also stored and transmitted securely, and that appropriate access controls are in place to prevent unauthorized access to the generated data.

4. Privacy: ChatGPT can process and generate personal data, it's important to ensure that the model is not used to generate data that could be used to identify or track individuals, and that appropriate privacy controls are in place to prevent the unauthorized use of personal data.

5. Compliance: ChatGPT can process and generate sensitive information, so it's important to ensure that the model and the data used to train and fine-tune the model comply with applicable data protection regulations, such as GDPR and CCPA.

6. Transparency: If ChatGPT is used to generate data in a business setting, it's important to ensure that the model's decision-making process is transparent, and that the model's decision can be audited and explained.

Overall, it's important to consider the security and privacy implications of ChatGPT when working with the model, and to implement appropriate controls to protect sensitive information.

Chapter 10: Best practices for using ChatGPT

When using ChatGPT, there are several best practices to keep in mind in order to achieve optimal performance and avoid common pitfalls:

1. Use high-quality, diverse, and unbiased training data: ChatGPT is only as good as the data it is trained on, so it's important to use high-quality, diverse, and unbiased data to improve the model's performance and reduce bias.
2. Fine-tune the model on specific tasks or domains: Fine-tuning the model on specific tasks or domains allows the model to learn the specific characteristics of the task and generate more accurate and relevant responses.
3. Use appropriate evaluation metrics: Use the appropriate evaluation metrics for the specific task, such as accuracy for classification tasks or BLEU score for machine translation tasks.

4. Continuously monitor the model's performance: ChatGPT is a machine learning model, and its performance may change over time. It's important to continuously monitor the model's performance and make adjustments as needed.

5. Use appropriate privacy and security controls: ChatGPT can process and generate sensitive information, so it's important to ensure that the model and the data used to train and fine-tune the model are stored and transmitted securely, and that appropriate access controls are in place to prevent unauthorized access.

6. Be transparent: If ChatGPT is used to generate data in a business setting, it's important to ensure that the model's decision-making process is transparent and that the model's decision can be audited and explained.

7. Consider ethical and compliance issues: ChatGPT can process and generate sensitive information, so it's important to ensure that the model and the data used to train and fine-tune the model comply with

applicable data protection regulations, such as GDPR and CCPA.

8. Use Explainable AI techniques: Since ChatGPT is a deep learning model, it can be difficult to understand how it generates its output. To mitigate this issue, it's important to use interpretable models, like decision trees, or use explainable AI techniques like LIME (Local Interpretable Model-Agnostic Explanations)

By following these best practices, you can ensure that you are using ChatGPT effectively and efficiently while also addressing ethical and compliance.

Chapter 11: Tips and Tricks for fine-tuning ChatGPT

Here are a few tips and tricks that can be used to improve the performance of fine-tuned ChatGPT models:

1. Use a smaller batch size: Using a smaller batch size when fine-tuning the model can help to prevent overfitting and improve the model's performance on the specific task.
2. Use a smaller learning rate: A smaller learning rate can help to prevent the model from overshooting the optimal solution during training.
3. Use a smaller number of training steps: A smaller number of training steps can help to prevent the model from overfitting to the training data.
4. Use early stopping: Early stopping can be used to prevent the model from overfitting by stopping the training when the model's performance on a held-out validation set stops improving.

5. Use a smaller model: A smaller model may require less computational resources and may be more suitable for fine-tuning on specific tasks or datasets with limited data.

6. Use a larger fine-tuning dataset: A larger fine-tuning dataset can help to improve the model's performance on the specific task by providing the model with more examples to learn from.

7. Use a pre-training task-specific dataset: Pre-training on a task-specific dataset can help the model to learn the characteristics of the task, and fine-tuning on a smaller dataset can then be done with better performance.

8. Use ensemble methods: Using ensemble methods like using a combination of multiple models or using a combination of multiple outputs from the same model can lead to better

Chapter 12: Advanced Applications of ChatGPT

ChatGPT can be used for a wide range of natural language processing (NLP) tasks, and here are a few advanced applications of the model:

1. Dialogue systems: ChatGPT can be used to create dialogue systems that can understand and respond to user inputs in a more natural way. This can be used for creating chatbots, virtual assistants, or interactive fiction.
2. Text summarization: ChatGPT can be fine-tuned to extract the most important information from a piece of text and condense it into a shorter version. This can be used in applications such as news summarization, document summarization, or meeting minutes.
3. Text classification: ChatGPT can be fine-tuned to classify text into different categories, such as sentiment analysis, topic classification, or intent identification.

4. Text generation with Constraints: ChatGPT can be fine-tuned to generate text that meets certain constraints, such as a specific length, style, or format. This can be used for applications such as poetry generation or text completion.

5. Language Modeling with Control: ChatGPT can be fine-tuned to generate text that meets certain control, such as specific words or phrases, or certain characteristics like the gender, tone, or style of the text.

6. Text-to-Speech: ChatGPT can be fine-tuned to generate synthetic speech, which can be used in applications such as speech synthesis, text-to-speech, or audio-based conversation systems.

7. Multimodal Language Processing: ChatGPT can be used in combination with other models such as image captioning, video captioning, or speech recognition to create multimodal language processing systems.

8. Adversarial Training: ChatGPT can also be used in adversarial training, where the model is trained to resist attacks from malicious inputs, such as text that is designed to fool the model into making

incorrect predictions. This can be used to improve the robustness and security of ChatGPT-based systems.

9. Generative Pre-training: ChatGPT can be used in generative pre-training, where the model is first trained to generate text, then fine-tuned on specific tasks, such as language translation, text classification, or question answering. This can improve the performance of the fine-tuned models.

10. Language Translation: ChatGPT can be fine-tuned to translate text from one language to another. This can be used in applications such as customer service, e-commerce or global content creation.

11. Language Modeling in Low-Resource Languages: ChatGPT can be fine-tuned on low-resource languages, where there is limited data available for training. This can be used to improve the performance of NLP tasks in these languages.

12. Machine Reading Comprehension: ChatGPT can be fine-tuned to answer questions based on a given text, a task also known as machine reading comprehension.

13. Language Modeling in Code: ChatGPT can be fine-tuned to generate code in a specific programming language, which can be useful for tasks such as code completion, code generation, or code formatting.

Overall, ChatGPT is a versatile and powerful language model that can be used for a wide range of natural language processing tasks, and these advanced applications demonstrate the flexibility and potential of the model.

Chapter 13: ChatGPT and Explainable AI

Explainable AI (XAI) is an area of research that aims to make the decision-making process of deep learning models more transparent and interpretable. Since ChatGPT is a deep learning model, it can be difficult to understand how it generates its output. Therefore, using XAI techniques can be useful when working with ChatGPT.

Here are a few XAI techniques that can be used with ChatGPT:

1. LIME (Local Interpretable Model-Agnostic Explanations): LIME is a technique that can be used to understand the predictions made by ChatGPT by approximating the model locally with an interpretable model, such as a linear model, and explaining the predictions in terms of the input features.

2. Attention visualization: Attention visualization is a technique that can be used

to understand which parts of the input are most important for the model's predictions. This can be used to understand why ChatGPT generates a particular output.

3. Counterfactual analysis: Counterfactual analysis is a technique that can be used to understand how small changes to the input would change the model's predictions. This can be used to understand the model's decision-making process and identify potential biases.

4. Model distillation: Model distillation is a technique that can be used to train a smaller, more interpretable model that mimics the behavior of ChatGPT. This can be used to understand the model's decision-making process without the need to interpret the large and complex ChatGPT model.

5. SHAP (SHapley Additive exPlanations): SHAP is a unified approach to explain the output of any machine learning model. It connects optimal credit allocation with local explanations using the classic Shapley

values from cooperative game theory to obtain individual feature importance values.

Using XAI techniques can help to make the decision-making process of ChatGPT more transparent and interpretable, which can be useful for understanding the model's behavior and identifying potential issues, such as bias or errors.

Chapter 14: ChatGPT and Fairness and Bias

Language models like ChatGPT are trained on large amounts of text data, which can reflect the biases present in the data.

For example, if a language model is trained on a dataset that contains biased language, it will likely generate biased language as well. This can lead to issues of fairness and bias in the model's output.

It is important for researchers to be aware of these issues and to take steps to mitigate bias in the training data and in the model itself.

This can include using diverse and balanced training data, as well as techniques such as debiasing or counterfactual data augmentation during the training process.

Additionally, it's recommended to evaluate the model on diverse test sets and diverse use-cases to ensure that the model is fair and unbiased.

However, it's important to note that the model is only a reflection of the data it was trained on, it's not a conscious entity that can be held responsible for any bias.

Therefore, it's important to also address the root causes of bias in data collection and curation.

Chapter 15: ChatGPT and Human-in-the-loop

A human-in-the-loop system is one in which a human and a machine (such as ChatGPT) work together to accomplish a task.

The human provides input, such as feedback or oversight, while the machine performs the bulk of the work.

This type of system can be used in a variety of applications, such as natural language processing, image recognition, and decision-making.

The goal of a human-in-the-loop system is to combine the strengths of both the human and the machine to improve the overall performance of the system.

Conclusion

ChatGPT is a highly versatile and already super-powerful A.I. system that is only going to get better and even more versatile in the coming months and years.

The bullet-pointed list below is merely the tip of the iceberg as to what ChatGPT is capable of:

1. ChatGPT can be used to generate natural language conversational AI agents.
2. It can be deployed on websites and mobile apps.
3. It can be used to interact with customers and answer customer queries.
4. It can be used to create virtual assistants for customer service.
5. It can be used to give a personalized customer experience.
6. It can provide proactive customer support.
7. It can automate mundane tasks like customer onboarding.
8. It can provide useful product recommendations.
9. It can generate customized sales pitches.

10. It can create interactive tutorials.

11. It can give valuable insights on customer behaviour.

12. It can be used to build marketing campaigns around customer conversations.

13. It allows integration with third-party services like Slack, Facebook Messenger, and Telegram.

14. It can be used to automate customer surveys and feedback.

15. It can be used to generate automated reports and summaries.

16. It can be used to develop AI-powered chatbots for customer service.

17. It can be used to generate customer responses to inquiries.

18. It can be used to create more engaging messaging experiences.

19. It can be used to understand customer preferences in order to personalize interactions.

20. It can be used to develop intelligent conversation analytics for better decision-making.

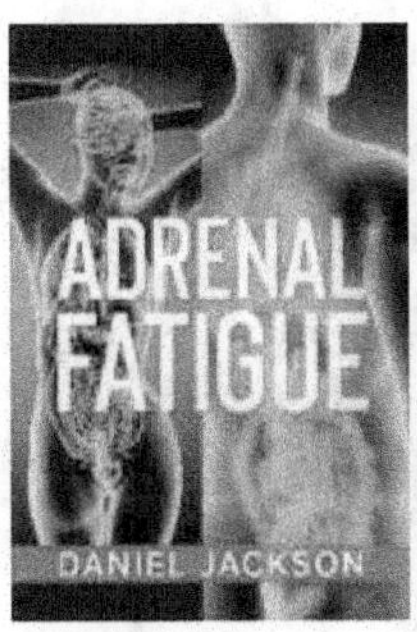

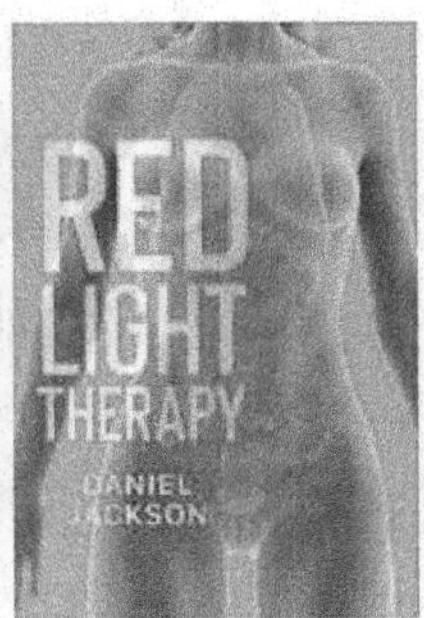

Take a look at more great books available from Rockwood Publishing

… **some for FREE!**

Just visit the link below:

rockwoodpublishing.co.uk

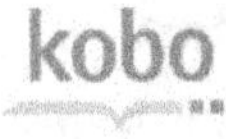

website links does not necessarily imply a recommendation or endorse the views expressed within them. Rockwood Publishing takes no responsibility for, and will not be liable for, the websites being temporarily unavailable or being removed from the Internet. The accuracy and completeness of information provided herein and opinions stated herein are not guaranteed or warranted to produce any particular results, and the advice and strategies contained herein may not be suitable for every individual. The author shall not be liable for any loss incurred as a consequence of the use and application, directly or indirectly, of any information presented in this work. This publication is designed to provide information in regards to the subject matter covered. The information included in this book has been compiled to give an overview of the subject(s) and detail some of the symptoms, treatments etc. that are available to people with this condition. It is not intended to give medical advice. For a firm diagnosis of your condition, and for a treatment plan suitable for you, you should consult your doctor or consultant. The writer of this book and the publisher are not responsible for any damages or negative consequences following any of the treatments or methods highlighted in this book. Website links are for informational purposes and should not be seen as a personal endorsement; the same applies to the products detailed in this book. The reader should also be aware that although the web links included were correct at the time of writing, they may become out of date in the future.